ECHOLOCATION

Sally Bliumis-Dunn

a plume editions book
AN IMPRINT OF MADHAT PRESS
ASHEVILLE, NORTH CAROLINA

MadHat Press
MadHat Incorporated
PO Box 8364, Asheville, NC 28814

The Library of Congress has assigned
this edition a Control Number of
2017951759

ISBN 978-1-941196-55-7 (paperback)

Text by Sally Bliumis-Dunn
Cover image & design by Wendy Letven

Plume Editions
an imprint of MadHat Press
www.MadHat-Press.com

First Printing

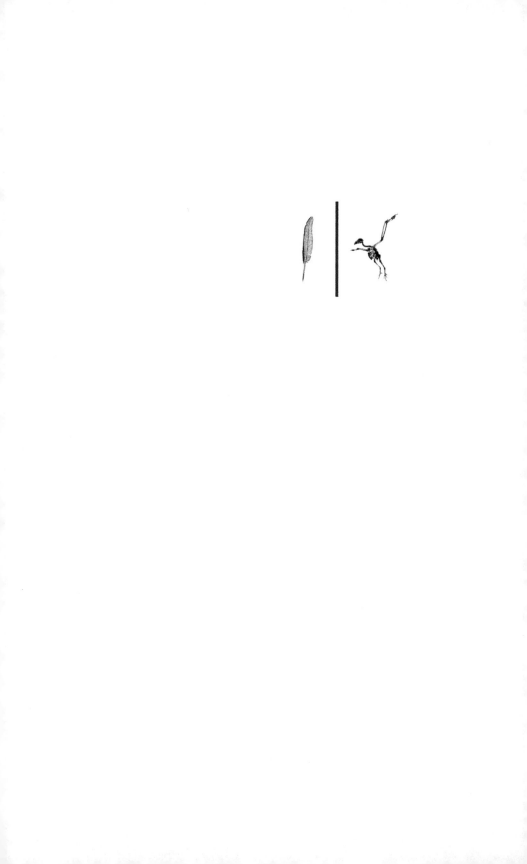

ECHOLOCATION

For my mother

Were it not for the way you taught me to look
at the world, to see the life at play in everything,
I would have to be lonely forever.

—Ted Kooser

Table of Contents

III.

IV.

Echolocation

The whales can't hear each other calling
in the noise-cluttered sea: they beach themselves.
I saw one once—heaved onto the sand with kelp
stuck to its blue-gray skin.
Heavy and immobile,

it lay like a great sadness.
And it was hard to breathe with all the stink.
Its elliptical black eyes had stilled, were mostly dry,
and barnacles clustered on its back
like tiny brown volcanoes.

Imagining the other whales, their roving weight,
their blue-black webbing of the deep,
I stopped knowing how to measure my own grief.
And this one, large and dead on the sand,
with its unimaginable five-hundred-pound heart.

I.

Holding

Pencil jar on the desk,
nail locked in the wall,
out the window, trees
cradle the sky.
Inside me, my mother,
age hooding her eyes,
my father, with less
and less to say, never mind
how long he's dead.

Sally Bliumis-Dunn

Mother

Little stirrings
in the dried fallen leaves along the path,
as when I speak to my old mother, and her eyes
widen for a moment then close.

She sits in her chair,
tweed jacket, well-coiffed,
looking as she did in her day,

though now someone else must dress her,
lift the blouse from the hanger,
help her slip it on,

the way she once did
for me. *Grab the cuff,* she'd say.
The soft tunnel of sleeve
would hold me.

Sometimes we sing.
She only vaguely mouths the words,
though occasionally she'll drift
along on a note like a leaf lifted by wind

before it stills.
If I sit by her on the couch
she'll put her head near mine,
my hand in hers.

Her body is how
she remembers now,
the way the growth of a tree,
the twists of its branches, recall
the rain, the snow, the sun.

Sally Bliumis-Dunn

Half Dome, Yosemite

When I learned the granite fell
in gigantic convex layers

and that this falling away
was what had formed the dome,

I thought of your palms
curved against my cheeks

when I was small.
And how at some point

you would know
to lower them

by your sides.

We Were Our Father's Second Family

Bright rectangles on the living room wall
where pictures must have hung,
we slept in their old rooms.
And outside the old homestead,

a black cast-iron hitching post
though we owned no horses; round white
millstones like giant moons held down
in the overgrown meadow.

Father's past in our present—
sometimes we'd sense it poking through
the gravelly chop of his voice—
the tall grass in the fields

bending toward it, the shadows
beneath the blades.

Sally Bliumis-Dunn

Heart Attack

Our father left us with his heart—
by then, a pale weak thing we never got
to tend before he died;

it hung in the bright air
like an abandoned nest,

and it is useless
to be sad, though I am sad—
above the fields,

yellow-edged wings—
an aubergine mourning cloak.
My father would have shown me

how to pinch its thorax, pin it
on the spreading board and wait

as if it would be less dead, more
enshrined in my own hands.

What's Left to Us

He'd come to her that morning,
a giant hummingbird whirring.

She could tell it was male
by the bright green wings.

And she knew
by the way it vanished—

the same flourish in the air
that her father had added

to his "y's," blue ink
drying on the pad,

fountain pen resting
in the folds of his hand.

With the bird gone,
she knew—

wasn't surprised to hear
her mother's voice

unsteady on the phone,
like someone wading

across a brook
balancing on stones.

Sally Bliumis-Dunn

Darwin's Finches

Brown dust or volcanic
ash, pieces of earth come alive,
they take quick flight,
blend back in with the brush.
In his many notebooks,
just a line or so about these birds
who might have remained
unremarked upon, their songs
dull as tarnished spoons.

Ars Poetica

At the kitchen table my brother
would crisp the folded lines, taper them
to a point at the airplane's tip.

The careful square flaps he knew
to tear on each side of the tail
allowed the plane's sudden dip

and slow flat sail to a flawless
landing on our red linoleum floor.
Though he tried to teach me,

mine flew poorly,
so I learned to sit and watch

as now I watch these arctic terns,
perfect paper planes,
falling from the sky, aimed

at floating crabs, with the precision
of mother's embroidery needle
piercing the cloth—

another quiet task
I could never master.

Sally Bliumis-Dunn

Visitation

For a moment, I had her attention,
faint as a moth's weight,
its hair-thin legs brushing the center of my palm;

then, as the moth lifted into jagged flight,
her eyes closed again, and from her mouth she breathed
a flurry of moths,

shredding the air,
like so many reckless scissors;
and they do not stop and will not land

as though she were a woolen sweater they had done with—
Damn moths, she used to say

when she brought the cedar box
down from the attic. And now they were leaving her,
woolen bits in their mothy guts.

Iron Latch

I do imagine it—
the coming back
to her house, after—

iron latch
on the old black door
colder beneath my thumb,

the iron hinges, keening,
the air, unbreathed,
stirring—

in the front hall, the mirror
where she'd glance and wink
before she left,

as though a truer self
stayed behind.

Then one last time
to my old room,
the cherry banister
leading.

II.

What's Missing

I have been cut loose and orbit,
wild, am not in sync with any moon,
as when I was a child, though back then
I would not have known the force

of women, living in a single house,
our periods aligned like vases on a window sill,
would not have shown an outward quiet,
as after heavy snow, its buffering walls

as I rode the tunnels to work
or tended a sick child,
all the while a wrecking ball
swinging loose inside me.

And now, moon, you appear
like a mouth, wide open.

Sally Bliumis-Dunn

"Aesthetics to Change the Way You Live"

—*Growth Magazine*

For instance, *wabi sabi*
a Japanese view of life
that celebrates the imperfect,

the light-hearted sound
of the two words
like figures balanced on a seesaw,

behind them, cloudless sky,
and in the spread, the photograph
of nicked and dulled silver spoons

arranged in rows on lilac velvet—
how perfectly imperfect.
Separate from the printed page,

the air around me darkens—
and then the sound
like thunder pressing closer

as I think of my own flaws—
and then they all
come charging toward me,

a herd of bison
so dense it's hard to see
from all the dust kicked up.

So loud I cannot think.
How much easier to be won over
by a living room's worn rug,

the reds and blues, faded,
even threadbare, in those places
I most often stand.

Sally Bliumis-Dunn

Flush

The lava lizard, chinless, reddens
at her throat to woo the male—

our own mother's neck would flush,
as though a vestige of that gene,

at any hint of sex. She would color—
a fine fishnet visible on her face and throat—

when my brother came home past curfew
or Dad's hand would linger
on the inlet of her apron's waist—

she'd still like a lizard's stare,
as if wishing she could just blend in
with the rock or the wall behind her.

Pregnant at the Beach

My mother could take anything—
stitches on the knee,
emergency appendectomy—

and bleach out
the colors—blood-reds, blues—
until there was nothing left

of the hospital room
but a lavender vase
on a mahogany table.

When she told me
that she didn't remember
any pain in childbirth,

I laid out my beach towel
on the soft sounds of her words,
my friends' tales of labor

like freighters in the distance—
didn't remember
any pain. And I lay there

basking, eyes closed.

Sally Bliumis-Dunn

While We Weren't Talking about Masturbation

I could feel the split
when my mother looked
in the rearview and told me

that I should wait until I was older
for feelings I'd already had during "naps."
I leaned forward,

tapped her shoulder with that same hand,
the backs of my six-year-old thighs
sticking to the red leather seats.

I was surprised I could
turn the window's metal crank
when she asked me to open it for air.

She talked on and on
about the beauty parlor,
ice cream at Schrafft's.

For a few moments
I couldn't speak,
my words obediently

wandering off to find that place
in the future I should wait for.

Mid-Winter

Bless those early years.
We still thought she could
save us, her hidden cave
unnoticed by our father. She soothed
us there with her soft paws—backrub
after night terror, the scrape of pacing
above us. She licked
our wounds with wordless
tongue, invisible
animal in her mid-calf quilted robe.

Sally Bliumis-Dunn

Startled

Massive and black,
the frigate birds
on brambles in the distance.

Their bright red gular sacs,
full as spinnaker sails,
billow from their feathers

like giant hearts of skin and air.
They remind us of our own

hearts, oversized and awkward,
quivering in the lightest wind.

Mechanics

When the engine light flashes
two days after an oil change,
I want to trust him—

after all, he once
fixed the headlamp,
no charge. I see

his garage from my office window,
and in the driveway,
a couple of oil-stained plastic chairs.

All set, he says, and I want
to trust him, but catch
myself in the car shop's mirror,

that old expression, like a door always
almost closed.
He says it's the coil—

something wound
come loose and leaking inside
the engine's metallic husk.

Car on the hydraulic lift,
he points, I nod
at the tubular dark.

Sally Bliumis-Dunn

For the Child Molester

Let him sleep right through it—
thin syringe, everlasting injection.

Then let it hang
like an old wool sock in a closet.

Let him wake like a child
from night terror,
clatter down the stairs,

rush to the toilet
reach for himself with shaking
thumb and forefinger
around the soft base of the shaft.

Let him not even sense the warmth
of urine as it leaves him.

Let him feel like he's touching
a soft dead bird
in that gray bathroom light.

Let him hunger for his hunger
the rest of his life.

Fable

Her mother calls her Long Ears,
but for the girl, that's not light-hearted—

too many family secrets
she wishes she did not know. They menace

like the shadows of a raptor's wings
that trail her through the field grass,

she with her bright white cotton tail
like a fallen cloud.

Sally Bliumis-Dunn

Sunflower

Tiny florets,
hundreds of them

elegantly posed
like miniature ballerinas

stuck in the flower's
large round center,

counting the steps of the sun
with their yellow tongues,

so small
you cannot see them,

and softly—
you will not hear them,

counting, obsessive
through the night,

afraid to lose
the rhythm.

Diminution

She served clichés like some mothers offered cake—
the hackneyed phrase edged right on through;
I still can hear her say,
just sowing his wild oats, as though that could excuse

the wrong. She'd drop us and our worries in
the drab room of generic phrase, and disappear—
the early bird, the dead horse beaten,
the leopard spots, those walls with ears.

Did she believe—she did, I think—the right
cliché could save us, help us not to feel
alone, so many bees in that same hive—
spilt milk, sow's ear, Achilles heel.

I miss them now that she is frail.
Her words these days, so spare, so plain.

Fable

She strains for air
gape-mouthed, eyes closed
with the hunger of a hatchling.
She throws off the covers,
limbs like twigs, hands stiff
like branches coated in ice,
no longer able to feel the air.
When the daughter tries to warm them,
she feels locked in furrowed bark,
as though she too
had been made part tree
by fate of filial vow
and was turning, even now
in her nest-like chair
by her mother's bed,
into something
wet-feathered, open-mouthed.

A Cutting

Back when I was seven,
you offered me a cutting—

I could not imagine
white nubs appearing

then growing into roots
that float as an old crone's hair

might float in the bath,
scraggly, tangled—

not like your auburn bangs,
the only part of you unchanged,

talisman of the mother we knew,
oilier, softer

from our hands
as we stroked your forehead

your last days.
I could not imagine.

We gathered by your bed
and your hair felt

like the fine-spun silk
of your evening jacket—

swans and little boatmen
swirling in the blue.

I could not imagine,
back when I was seven,

and you cut the fattest stem
from your favorite plant

with its big magenta heart
centering each leaf,

and you placed it in a glass of water
telling me it will grow.

Loon

Her feathers like the herringbone
tweed our mother wore,

matching scarf over solid black—
I watch her paddle around,

small chicks on her back,
her mate not far away on their nest

in the lakeside grass
turned yellow in late August.

I swim closer, quiet breaststroke,
and though she does not see me

as I break the surface,
cool wind on my face,

I hear the startling call as though
from a place of longing

in the summer air that our mother
no longer feels against her skin.

III.

Drive

Driving through a little town,
in front of a drugstore,
a girl skips rope. I watch her
jumping up and down
inside the perfect oval, the safe egg
the pink rope makes—
the hood of our Honda,
the upturned hull of my heart.
We drive through the world
as it quietly falls apart.
I don't know how to help my child.
The gray highway like a dead river,
how is it we continue to move?
The leaves are maple, mostly yellow.
They do not fall like rain.
It is late. We should stop
and eat before it turns dark,
but we don't.

Sally Bliumis-Dunn

Clue

In the drift   of those first days
when time had not yet settled

    into your infant body,
    I saw you as a young boy.

You never wore
the pin-striped uniform   that I imagined,
    or posed, bat in hand, on our lawn.

Slowly, like an old letter,
handwriting worn away
where the stationery folds,
I reopen that early vision of you, carefully

run my fingers through the grass
           where you might have stood,
as though there might be something

important but small there—

    a ring, a coin, a tarnished pin.

Pond

Metallic rain
cuts into

the pond's banks,
each day, a little deeper.

The clear
watery blades.

Each hour,
widening cracks,

loosened rocks
tumble.

This is where
the sadness goes.

This is how
it tunnels the body.

Sally Bliumis-Dunn

After

A cow's hind flank,
its small geography
of sinew and bone could fascinate
the boy who had not shown

much interest in paintbrush or clay
before the blow to his head
from the heavy wooden swing
that day we all stood watching.

The nurse ran out.
Teachers hurried us inside.
Weeks until he returned,
sullen, quieter.

He sculpted cows and pigs,
so detailed we saw patches
where their hides had matted or thinned,
so real we could almost see

the unprotected pink
skin showing through—
this change within
a boy we thought we knew

made us all unsteady.
The white chalk numbers, their simple
additions and subtractions, hid
a more complicated truth.

Quahogue

Along the shore like white eyelids,
bleached dead clams.
I see one that is alive.
I stop and watch it open
the two locked lids of its dull shell,
let emerge a delicate foot,
like a white peony petal
that lifts the grains of sand,
burying itself, until what's left
is a pucker on the tidal flats, pulsing.
The sand is freckled with many such holes,
and I feel let in on a secret
as when I caught the scraps
of your voice and I knocked
and you showed me the letter
from your father who left when you were five.
And you told me that you read it,
sometimes aloud, its white rectangle a door
you keep open like a clam's thin syphon.

Sally Bliumis-Dunn

Octopus

Soft flower,
reddish-brown
floating, petals open
for a moment
before it folds
its body tight,
closed bud
propels itself
to the sandy bottom
where it blanches,
entirely blends in;
only a ruffle
of suckered leg rustles
beneath the sand.

She

Her hair the gray
of hungry squirrels

stitching the wet snow,
wind in crests of winter trees

rocking them like wicker cradles—
so many years behind her now,

and voices no longer fly to her
like grackles to an open field.

She used to admire the striations
of their blue-black feathers

tapering towards the tails that bobbed
slightly as they sang.

The loons on the bay
that blur now at short distance.

The tall bare oaks that moan
their losses. She envies them

their spring.

Sally Bliumis-Dunn

Menopause

The iris of the Galapagos dove
turns blue when ready for mating,
like the painted eyes of preteen girls

when vials of shadow and tint
migrate from the drugstore
to their bathroom counters.

Part genetic code
which urges them along.
This goes on for years,

until, like me, they feel,
even as they primp and preen,
that a hand

has dropped away
from where it had been pressing, warm
on the small of the back—

so much a part of the self
that it hadn't been missed
until now.

How Your Dress Was Made

Wooden bobbins, hanging
like a miniature suspension bridge—

lace patterns pinned to pillows,
the many threads, a thick mist—

each day, your wedding,
a world I enter, bedazzled as a child.
Today, a bridge in white

mountains, a Chinese painting,
snow silver—freshly fallen.

Nest

I admire them for days,
carrying bits in their tweezer beaks,
this pair of blue-gray phoebes.

Lichen threads and moss.
They weave the air with their work,
the nest so green it could be

growing under the eaves.
String, clay, and spit.
Maybe some strands of my hair?

In the chemistry of our mingling—
she won't allow me near.
Each time I open the sliding door,

she startles to a nearby pine—abandons
the three white eggs
she had warming beneath her.

Beets

Watch for the shoulders of the beets to protrude above the soil.
—Farmer's Almanac

Yes to the shoulders
of the beets.
An upward tug on red-veined leaves—
as if might follow miniature
torsos, legs, and feet.
Today, I rescue them
as men I've loved.
Because for a moment,
in this guise,
they can all
be good.

Sally Bliumis-Dunn

Sea Turtles Mating

His under-shell, concave,
makes it easy to lock on;
we watch from the boat,

the island of volcanic ruff
in jagged silhouette behind us.

They push through water
like a plough
through weighty snow,

he, mostly still; she
paddles them along,
sometimes a full six hours
till he slides off.

To be amazed at her luck
or pity her trials—

I look for signs
and see none,
her hooked mouth

closed, her green eyes
unchanging.

IV.

White-tipped Reef Shark

Let the slow whip of its body
kick up smallish clouds
along the sandy bottom—

a little atmosphere down there,
clouds, plants. Let there even be a sun.

Let the shark stay far away
as we swim the shaken surface.

Let it be its own small country,
the white tip on the dorsal fin, a flag of peace

that will hold in check
inward-pointing teeth,
hard wedge of jaw,

dark holes of the sunken eyes
that close when it strikes.

Sally Bliumis-Dunn

The Night I Dreamed You Died

A swan falling
from the sky, on fire.
Flames rush
towards its orange beak.
I must have woken quickly.
The neck and head
were still white.

Flight 214

The news is still falling
in our kitchen
like invisible rain

as we eat the pink salmon,
the lettuce, the mashed potatoes.

Because now everything
glistens. The candles, the soft

folds of red napkins
each in its place,

as though it all were sacred—
the rain
must still be falling.

Not me, not anyone I know.

Earlier in the day, the terrible
news lifted too easily,

a cheap Mylar balloon
cut loose—a tinny flash.

Couldn't even tell its color
against the sky.

Sally Bliumis-Dunn

Titanic

Some of the shoes
still lie in pairs

on the ocean floor.
Small slender boats—

the flirtatious tilt
of an ankle in a t-strap,

glare of chandelier
on a shiny oxford,

the broken clocks
of bodies swaying.

Knots

The briny knotted rope
let out over the transom

through the curled fingers
of that first sailor's
rough and reddened hands.

When I read *seven knots*
on our small digital screen,
blue Caribbean sky
cupping us in its palm,

I imagine the careful knots
along that first rope's braided length
as we eye the coast for port.

Just another word, lifting
up from where it came,
like all of those tiny peaks of waves,
then going back down.

Sally Bliumis-Dunn

Returning

First time since the accident—
     the tree, half-standing,
seems to hold

     in its snap-jagged trunk
the moments of just after,
though it's been months.

We spot flowers,
         white blossoms

the size of a thumbnail,
    stems a few inches tall.

Oh to be small enough
to follow white flowers
like old-fashioned street lamps

lighting the village
after dark.

Work

I could tell they were father and son,
the air between them slack, as though
they hardly noticed one another.

The father sanded the gunwales,
the boy coiled the lines.
And I admired them there, each to his task

in the quiet of the long familiar.
The sawdust coated the father's arms
like dusk coats grass in a field.

The boy worked next on the oarlocks
polishing the brass until it gleamed,
as though he could harness the sun.

Who cares what they were thinking,
lucky in their lives
that the spin of the genetic wheel

slowed twice to a stop
and landed each of them here.

Sally Bliumis-Dunn

Anagramming

Silent, the word

lifting off, only
its letters

in the white air
of the page, swirl,

rearrange,
then brighten

as though at dawn,
a flock of robins

struggling to gather
in the wind;

anagram's answer
lands on the lawn,

brown heads lowered
into thin spring blades.

For burrowing worms,
hear, *listen.*

Golden Stingrays

Like giant yellow leaves
sunk through the heavy water,

they revive on the bottom—
as though the sea
conferred on them

another life
when they could sink
no further.

Sally Bliumis-Dunn

Berlin

We see the public statues,
water-stained and darker now.
Small bullet scars on buildings—

how can it be so quiet?
Though I keep almost hearing
someone close behind me,

the footsteps, voices
traveling toward me,
and I am in a dog's world

without the dog's keen hearing.
I have only my sad psyche
where rounded cobblestones

appear like tops of shaven heads
and underneath,
the rest of their clothed bodies

cramped into a crowd
mercilessly, still standing.

Glasswing Butterfly

Wings like windows,
we look through them—
                a glasswing feeds

on lantana's orange parasol,
                    resting on a flower.

We shift through rooms,
heavy in ourselves,
              in our things.

Just the few black veins
on its wings
          threading it to this world.

Sally Bliumis-Dunn

Biopsy

Here on the cold examination table,
I miss the cradle of my bra.
Soon the radiologist will sink
a bright needle into my breast.

In the low afternoon light,
I envision a woman and a man
painted on a basilica's ceiling,
she in a red robe, he in muted brown.

The doctor positions my body on the table—
the woman becomes my mother,
red gown illuminated

by the light of her dressing table,
and the man, my father, waiting
for her in the blue plaster sky
that holds them.

Conversation

Green hummingbird,
head tilted into the deeper
orange of each blossom,

as if it were listening,
closely, again and again,
but could not hear

whatever it was trying to hear—
blossoms like slender gramophones,
pale notes of wings

beat the air—
all of that work steady
above the open blossom.

You with sharp ears
keep asking me,
What did you just say?

The trumpet vine
holds loosely to the trellis.

We are talking.
The hummingbirds
vanish, reappear.

Sally Bliumis-Dunn

Road Sign

Hard to keep watching the dull
forever of the road;
the orange and yellow leaves

will not stay like this, burning
the blue with their flat candles—

sitting by my grandmother's bed,
I'd watch the slow rise and fall

of sheets, afraid to look away
as though it mattered
which last breath of hers I saw.

Solstice

Invisible mountain of light.
Tomorrow we begin
the walk down.

Each day a little more.
Beautifully imprecise
instrument of the body—

it could be weeks
before we notice
the duller green of the maples,

the afternoon light tilting
like water in a glass.

Sally Bliumis-Dunn

Journal of Your Dying

Could you hear me

sometimes you grasped my hand

like soil draining itself of water
like roots still gripping—

both of these at once

*

words
like bats stuck upside down
in a cave they would never leave

your sweet mouth   open

Ode to Autumn

So many colors abandon the earth,
and go skyward to the trees
like origami birds,

scarlet, orange, creased
and folded into the mind
where these paper birds come alive,
the trees quiver a little—

this is where I can
still see you

in these gray branches
with brightly colored
birds that are not birds—envision you

still darning
the heels of Jimmy's socks
those evenings after school

at the kitchen table when
you'd run your finger down our list—

not here in the duller green
where the last of the pink roses
are browning on the vine,

and along the fence,
your favorite lilies, wilted,

and everywhere
the hungry bees.

Acknowledgments

The Academy of American Poets: "Flight 214," "Work," and "Echolocation"

The American Journal of Poetry: "After"

Connotation Press: "Mechanics"

Cortland Review: "Returning"

Galapagos Poems (Kattywompus Press, 2016): "Darwin's Finches," "Golden Stingrays," "Octopus," "Sea Turtles Mating," and "White-tipped Reef Shark"

Heron Tree: "The Night I Dreamed You Died"

Juxtaprose Literary Magazine: "Conversation"

New Ohio Review: "Aesthetics to Change the Way We Live"

Plume: "Titanic," "For the Child Molester," "Heart Attack," "Berlin," and "We Were Our Father's Second Family"

Salamander: "Biopsy"

The Same: "Sunflower"

Terrain: "Anagrammer"

upstreet: "Pond," "Flush"

Valparaiso Review: "Beets"

ABOUT THE AUTHOR

SALLY BLIUMIS-DUNN teaches Modern Poetry at Manhattanville College, Personal Essay at the 92nd Street Y and conducts individual manuscript conferences at the Palm Beach Poetry Festival. She received her B.A. in Russian language and literature from U.C. Berkeley in 1983 and her MFA in Poetry from Sarah Lawrence College in 2002. Her poems have appeared in The Academy of American Poets' Poem-a-Day, Ted Kooser's American Life in Poetry, *New Ohio Review, The New York Times, Nimrod,* the *Paris Review, PBS NewsHour, Plume, Poetry London, Prairie Schooner, Rattle, Verse Daily,* and Garrison Keillor's *The Writer's Almanac.* In 2002, she was a finalist for the *Nimrod*/Hardman Pablo Neruda Prize. Her first book, *Talking Underwater,* was published by Wind Publications in 2007. In 2008, she was asked to read in the "Love Poems Program" at the Library of Congress. Her second book, *Second Skin,* was published by Wind Publications in 2010. Her chapbook *Galapagos Poems* was published by Kattywompus Press in 2016. She lives in Armonk, New York, and Harpswell, Maine, with her husband, John. They share four children, Ben, Angie, Kaitlin and Fiona.

WORDS OF THANKS

I would like to thank my first readers, Judy Fletcher, Julie Raskin and Philip Warburg, who helped me sift through the miscellany of first drafts to see what might go on to become a second. And to my careful second readers, Marion Brown, Theresa Burns, Peggy Ellsberg, Joan Falk, Jennifer Franklin, Alison Jarvis, Judy Katz, June Stein, and Margo Stever. I am grateful to Frances Richey for helping me discover the narrative through line of these poems. And a gigantic thank-you to Danny Lawless and Marc Vincenz for inviting me to submit *Echolocation* to Plume Editions/ MadHat Press, and too for your wise and generous editorial counsel. I am grateful to Wendy Letven for the cover art, to Angela Bliumis for the author photo and to Ted Kooser for allowing me to quote from his poem "Mother" for the book's dedication.

CPSIA information can be obtained
at www.ICGtesting.com
Printed in the USA
FFHW02n1117210918
48489808-52340FF

As a series, the poems in *Echolocation* swing back and forth from the natural world keenly observed—rain, birds, sunflowers, even a clam— to the contortions of the human heart, mostly caused by hurt and loss. And isn't that where the best poetry resides, between the thing and the emotion, the swan and the grief?

—BILLY COLLINS

Echolocation is a collection driven by image and figurative language— often the simile—and Bliumis-Dunn has both power of observation and imagination which she uses to great, lovely, terrifying and always compelling effect in these vivid, near- and far-looking poems.

—MARTHA RHODES

Sally Bliumis-Dunn's spare and stunning lyrics of grief and loss restore us to the clarity, and the clear finality, of our deepest emotions. They are grave and formal while being at the same time almost unbearably human and intimate.

—VIJAY SESHADRI

Sally Bliumis-Dunn leaves the reader of *Echolocation* in deceptively complex verbal landscapes in which both literal and figurative language play off each other with spare yet lapidary results in poems that focus on such everyday subjects as family, animals, loss, the seasons, menopause, and disaster with a compassionate, distilling eye. The voice that emanates from these poems is quiet but deeply resonant with generous stirrings beneath. She writes with what John Keats has called "disinterestedness"—a clear-headed objectivity that combines lucid narrative with lyrical charge.

—CHARD DE NIORD

plume editions

an imprint of
MADHAT PRESS
ASHEVILLE, NC

MADHAT-PRESS.COM

$18
ISBN 978-1-941196-55
018

9 781941 196557

9781941196557   11/09
ECHOLOCATION   BLIUMIS-
22   Book Culture
221   Our Price: $18.